Wellbeing
Student's Book 5

William Collins' dream of knowledge for all began with the publication of his first book in 1819.

A self-educated mill worker, he not only enriched millions of lives, but also founded a flourishing publishing house. Today, staying true to this spirit, Collins books are packed with inspiration, innovation and practical expertise.

They place you at the centre of a world of possibility and give you exactly what you need to explore it.

Collins. Freedom to teach.

Published by Collins

An imprint of HarperCollins*Publishers*
The News Building, 1 London Bridge Street, London, SE1 9GF, UK

HarperCollins*Publishers*
Macken House, 39/40 Mayor Street Upper, Dublin 1 D01 C9W8

Browse the complete Collins catalogue at
collins.co.uk

British Library Cataloguing-in-Publication Data
A catalogue record for this publication is available from the British Library.

Cambridge International copyright material in this publication is reproduced under licence and remains the intellectual property of Cambridge Assessment International Education.

Third-party websites and resources referred to in this publication have not been endorsed by Cambridge International Education.

Endorsement indicates that a resource has passed Cambridge International Education's rigorous quality-assurance process and is suitable to support the delivery of a Cambridge curriculum framework. However, endorsed resources are not the only suitable materials available to support teaching and learning, and are not essential to achieve the qualification. Resource lists found on the Cambridge website will include this resource and other endorsed resources.

Any example answers to questions taken from past question papers, practice questions, accompanying marks and mark schemes included in this resource have been written by the authors and are for guidance only. They do not replicate examination papers. In examinations the way marks are awarded may be different. Any references to assessment and/or assessment preparation are the publisher's interpretation of the curriculum framework requirements. Examiners will not use endorsed resources as a source of material for any assessment set by Cambridge International Education.

While the publishers have made every attempt to ensure that advice on the qualification and its assessment is accurate, the official curriculum framework, specimen assessment materials and any associated assessment guidance materials produced by the awarding body are the only authoritative source of information and should always be referred to for definitive guidance.

Our approach is to provide teachers with access to a wide range of high-quality resources that suit different styles and types of teaching and learning.

For more information about the endorsement process, please visit www.cambridgeinternational.org/endorsed-resources

Series editors: Kate Daniels and Victoria Pugh
Authors: Kate Daniels and Victoria Pugh
Publisher: Elaine Higgleton
Product Manager: Cathy Martin
Product developer: Roisin Leahy
Development and copy editor: Jo Kemp
Proofreader: Claire Throp
Permissions researcher: Rachel Thorne
Illustrations: Jouve India Ltd.
Cover designer: Amparo Barrera, Kneath Associates and Gordon MacGilp
Typesetter: Sam Vail, Ken Vail Graphic Design
Production controller: Sarah Hovell
Printed and bound by Martins the Printers

MIX
Paper | Supporting responsible forestry
FSC www.fsc.org
FSC™ C007454

This book is produced from independently certified FSC™ paper to ensure responsible forest management.

For more information visit: www.harpercollins.co.uk/green|

Third-party websites and resources referred to in this publication have not been endorsed by Cambridge Assessment International Education.

Access and download editable versions of these resources and the accompanying PowerPoint presentations at collins.co.uk/internationalresources

We are grateful to the following teachers for providing feedback on the resources as they were developed:
Ms Hema Gehani and Ms Seema Desai at Colours Innovation Academy, Ms Manjari Tennakoon and Ms Surani Maithripala at Gateway Colleges, and Preeti Roychoudhury, Farishta Dastur Mukerji, Spriha Patronobis and Sukonna Halder at Calcutta International School.

Contents

Hello and welcome to Wellbeing Stage 5's student's book!

All feelings matter

As the new school year starts, we hope you feel confident and excited about the year ahead.

But don't worry if you feel a bit nervous too – that's okay. We all have a mix of feelings every single day.

This workbook aims to help you express and understand all your feelings. It is also packed with ways to help you feel better when you find life hard. There are so many things you can do to help yourself.

A strong mind

When you exercise your body through running and swimming, it gets stronger. When you exercise your mind, it gets stronger too.

Working through this workbook will help you feel more in control of your feelings and more confident about yourself.

Yes you can

As you work through this workbook you will learn some awesome things, such as:

- how to understand your feelings
- how to be a good friend
- how to keep safe

and all sorts of other helpful ways YOU CAN look after yourself and make life better.

It is amazing what you can do when you know how.

Are you ready to give it a go?

May your year ahead be as amazing as you are!

– *Becky Goddard-Hill*

Unit 5.1 Loss

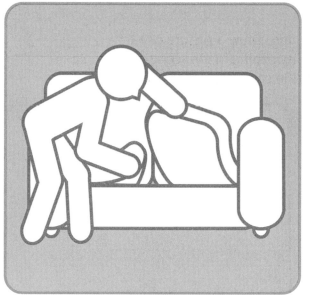

What do you know?

- What can you see in the pictures?
- Have you ever been in this situation?
- How did you feel?

In this unit, you will:

- Consider how people feel when they experience the loss of a person they love.
- Research the ways in which different cultures and religions celebrate a person's life when they have died.

Lesson 1 Losing something

Activity 1.1a Storyboard

Create a scenario where someone has lost something. Draw a picture of each freeze frame. Write a sentence to explain what is happening in the scene, then use key words or phrases to explain how each of the characters is feeling.

Lesson 1 Losing something

Activity 1.1b Emotion strategies mind map

Think about the ways in which you might be able to overcome some of the emotions that you experience when you lose something and can't get it back. For example, if you lose something that belongs to someone else you could apologise. Annotate the box below with examples of strategies.

What could I do?

Lesson 2 Losing someone we love

Activity 1.2a People you love

Think of some people you love in your life. What are your favourite things to do with them? How do you like to spend time together? Write down or draw some of the things you enjoy doing together below.

Lesson 2 Losing someone we love

Activity 1.2b Reflection

Write three key things you have learned from the lesson today.

1. _____
_____
_____
_____

2. _____
_____
_____
_____

3. _____
_____
_____
_____

Who or where could you go for support following loss/change?

_____
_____
_____
_____

What advice would you give to support a friend going through a similar change to Ayesha?

_____
_____
_____
_____

Lesson 3 Celebrating life in different cultures

Activity 1.3a Changes in our lives

What comes to mind when you think of the word 'change'?

Use the space below to create a mind map of everything you can think of regarding change in your life, in other's lives or in life around you.

Lesson 3 Celebrating life in different cultures

Activity 1.3b Reflection

List three things you have learned today about celebrating life around the world.

1. _____

_____

_____

_____

2. _____

_____

_____

_____

3. _____

_____

_____

_____

How is life celebrated in your own culture or religion?

Unit reflection

Think about what you have learned in this lesson and then write your own definitions of these words.

Grief – _____

_____

_____

_____

_____

_____

Loss – _____

_____

_____

_____

_____

_____

Celebration – _____

_____

_____

_____

_____

_____

Love – _____

_____

_____

_____

_____

_____

What do you know?

- What do you think is happening in the photo?
- How might the children be feeling?
- What is the child in the middle of the photo holding?

In this unit, you will:

- Consider why you are special and what you have achieved.
- Create your own edited photos.
- Explore a range of strategies to look after your mind.

Lesson 1 Celebrating achievements

Activity 2.1a My achievements

Think about something you are proud of or something you have achieved, and why you are proud of it.

Describe the achievement below. You can illustrate it if you would like to.

I am proud of _____

_____

_____

_____

_____

_____

_____

Lesson 1 Celebrating achievements

Activity 2.1b What types of achievements do people celebrate in life?

Work on your own or with a partner to draw and label achievements that people might celebrate.

Lesson 2 Images on the internet

Activity 2.2a Before and after pictures

Stick in your 'before' photo and then the edited 'after' photo.

Annotate all of the changes you made. Why did you make these changes?

Lesson 2 Images on the internet

Activity 2.2b How to support your positive self-esteem

What strategies can you think of to use to support your self-esteem and remind yourself how fantastic you are? Write your ideas to create a mind map below.

Lesson 3 Self-care

Activity 2.3a What is self-care?

What does self-care mean? Note your ideas in the balloons below. You can write sentences or words, or draw pictures you associate with self-care.

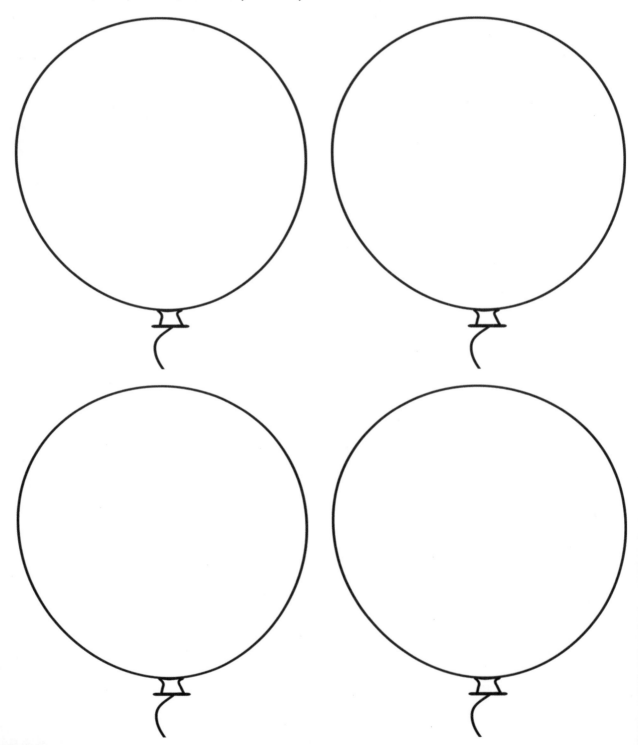

Lesson 3 Self-care

Activity 2.3b Keeping healthy

Think about all the ways you keep your body healthy and write them in the left-hand circle below. Now think about any ways you can keep your mind healthy and write them in the right-hand circle. If any are for both a healthy body and mind, write them in the middle where the two circles overlap.

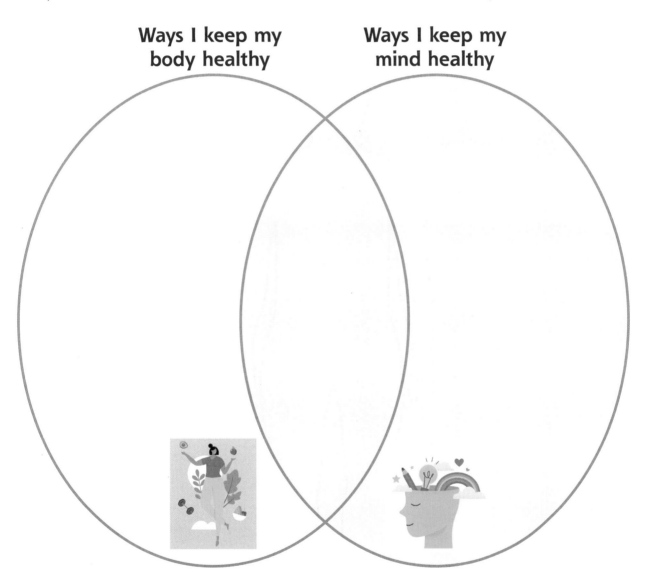

Ways I keep my body healthy

Ways I keep my mind healthy

Have you written anything in the section where the two circles overlap? Which things work for both body and mind?

_____

_____

_____

Unit reflection

What makes you, you?

Think about all of the things which make you who you are and write them around or inside the outline below.

Think about the roles you play with other people and the things you do. For example, you might be a big brother, a caring daughter, a talented chef or a fast runner. Don't forget to decorate the person below to look like you!

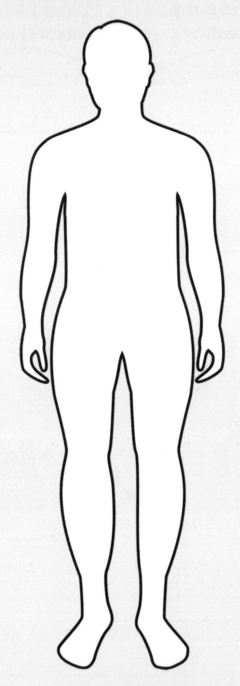

Unit 5.3 Habits to keep us healthy

What do you know?

- What are the people in these photos doing?
- Why might they be doing these things?

In this unit, you will:

- Learn about the importance of sleep.
- Find out what can help you to sleep better.
- Learn about the importance of sunlight, vitamin D and exercise for good physical and mental health.

Lesson 1 Time to sleep!

Activity 3.1a Sleep, sleep, sleep

Why might children like or dislike bedtime? Use the mind maps below to record your thoughts.

Dislike

Like

Lesson 1 Time to sleep!

Activity 3.1b Wordsearch

Can you find all the words in the box, which link to how you might feel if you don't get enough sleep?

f	o	r	g	e	t	f	u	l	n	e	s	s	w
a	x	s	o	f	o	w	o	j	t	x	l	c	i
t	y	r	k	e	y	g	u	n	s	h	e	q	n
i	a	m	d	d	h	r	h	h	g	a	e	u	a
g	s	j	w	h	n	u	g	e	a	u	p	v	t
u	g	y	o	e	r	m	u	n	s	s	y	z	t
e	a	u	g	a	a	p	v	d	k	t	b	w	e
h	f	r	t	d	c	y	a	w	n	i	n	g	n
t	i	m	p	a	t	i	e	n	t	o	m	p	t
h	y	g	s	c	y	a	p	g	r	n	j	l	i
s	e	s	h	h	i	z	s	c	a	k	v	b	o
h	q	j	c	e	m	o	t	i	o	n	a	l	n
s	c	o	b	s	r	m	s	u	f	q	y	w	g

Forgetfulness	**Impatient**
Yawning	**Fatigue**
Headaches	**Inattention**
Sleepy	**Grumpy**
Emotional	**Exhaustion**

Lesson 1 Time to sleep!

Activity 3.1c Why is sleep important?

List four reasons why sleep is important.

What is the difference between rest and sleep?

_____

Lesson 2 Getting to sleep

Activity 3.2a Bedtime routines

In the table below, write your current bedtime routine and the times that each part happens. There may be some days which are different and that is ok.

Time	Activity	Detail	How effective is this to help you to get to sleep?

What would you like to change about your current routine?

_____

_____

_____

_____

Lesson 2 Getting to sleep

Activity 3.2b Top five tips for an effective bedtime routine

Can you share your top five tips for creating an effective bedtime routine?

Top 5 list

1 _____

2 _____

3 _____

4 _____

5 _____

Lesson 3 Exercise and natural light

Activity 3.3 Exercise and vitamin D

Using a range of online sources and books from your library, research one of the following areas:

- Why vitamin D is important and how we can get more vitamin D.
- Why exercise is important for our body and mind.

Don't forget to record where you found the information so that you can check that they are reliable sources.

Information found	Source

Unit reflection

Consider what you have learned about the importance of good sleep, natural light and regular exercise to your physical and mental health. Write or draw your answers around the cloud to create a mind map.

Key things I have learned about the importance of sleep and exercise

What do you know?

- Why and how might relationships with friends and family change?
- How would you support a victim of bullying?
- Look at this picture. What does it mean to you? How could it relate to you and your family, friends or classmates?

In this unit, you will:

- Learn about different households.
- Understand changes in friendships.
- Consider how to support victims of bullying.

Lesson 1 Our families

Activity 4.1a My family

Sketch a picture of your family in the frame below. Put everyone in the picture: your family/people you live with, including any extended family or other people who live in your house.

You will use the notes section at the bottom of this page later – your teacher will tell you when.

Notes: Some interesting things about my family/people I live with (for example, hobbies, beliefs, customs, jokes, favourite food).

_____

_____

_____

_____

_____

Lesson 1 Our families

Activity 4.1b Reflection

What new things have you learned about your friends? How did learning these new things make you feel?

Lesson 2 Different friendships

Activity 4.2a My friendship map

Imagine your life as a path, from when you were born to how old you are now. Draw this path from the top to the bottom of this page. Then think about the friends you have had in your life and draw these friends on to your path. You don't have to draw all of them, just the ones who have been closest to you (you can just draw them as stick people or simple figures). Beside them, write their name and roughly how old you were when you met them.

Lesson 2 Different friendships

Activity 4.2b Reflection

1. What have you learned in this lesson?

_____

_____

_____

_____

_____

_____

_____

2. Think about your friendships now and since you were very little. How have they changed? How does this make you feel?

_____

_____

_____

_____

_____

3. How might they change in the future? How does this make you feel?

_____

_____

_____

_____

4. Is there anything you would like to find out more about or that you are worried about?

_____

_____

_____

Lesson 2 Different friendships

Activity 4.2c Making friends

Read these two extracts from Ammar's story in *The New Kid* and think about the different ways we make friends.

Everyone seemed to know each other well here. As the children chatted, Ammar felt even lonelier than he did at home. He wished he was at school in Syria with his best friend, Omar, playing football together in the playground.

The teacher said something, and everyone turned to Ammar. Ammar didn't understand what she'd said, so he stared at his shoes. He wanted to run and hide in the toilets, but he didn't even know where they were!

Later...

Ammar jumped when he felt a hand on his shoulder.

It was Tom. "You're really good at tennis!" he said. "Let's go and play! Come on!"

Had Ammar heard right? Did Tom say he was good? Ammar knew what that meant!

Tom put out a hand to help Ammar up and smiled. He said something else that Ammar couldn't understand, but it didn't matter. Ammar could tell he was being a good friend.

Lesson 3 Being a bystander

Activity 4.3 How to be an active bystander

Look carefully at the image above. Can you label the victim, the bystander and the person/people doing the bullying?

How could the bystander in this picture help the victim safely? List all the different ways you can think of.

_____

_____

_____

_____

_____

Is there anything that has worried you in this lesson or that you would like to know more about?

_____

_____

_____

Unit reflection

Think about all that you have learned and explain all the different ways you can be a better friend, family member and member of society.

- _____
  _____
  _____
  _____
  _____
  _____
  _____

- _____
  _____
  _____
  _____
  _____
  _____
  _____

- _____
  _____
  _____
  _____
  _____
  _____

- _____
  _____
  _____
  _____
  _____
  _____

Unit 5.5 Love

What do you know?
- What can you see in the picture?
- What do you think the heart symbolises?
- How do people express love?

In this unit, you will:
- Identify people that you love in your life.
- Create a family activity jar.

Lesson 1 Love is all around

Activity 5.1a Love, love, love

Who do you love? You can draw pictures or write in the hearts. Remember, they do not have to be family.

Lesson 1 Love is all around

Activity 5.1b Planning acts of love and kindness

Who are you planning to show an act of love and kindness to?

_____

_____

_____

What do they like and dislike?

_____

_____

_____

_____

_____

What will you do?

_____

_____

_____

_____

_____

_____

_____

How do you think they will respond?

_____

_____

_____

_____

_____

Lesson 2 Spending time together

Activity 5.2 Family activities

Draw or write about a time when you have enjoyed an activity with your family or people you love.

What made the activity so fun? How did you feel when you spent time with your family?

Lesson 3 Being part of a community

Activity 5.3a Kindness in my community

Consider what projects you could carry out to spread kindness within your community. Remember to listen to all of the ideas in your group and then decide on one to plan.

What we are going to do _____

_____

_____

_____

_____

_____

_____

_____

Why _____

_____

_____

_____

_____

_____

_____

What we will need and who will get it.

_____
_____
_____
_____
_____
_____
_____
_____
_____

How long it will take _____

Our plan

_____
_____
_____
_____
_____
_____
_____
_____
_____
_____
_____
_____
_____

Lesson 3 Being part of a community

Activity 5.3b Reflection

Reflect on what you think community means. Add words or phrases which you think are relevant to community to make a mind map below.

What is a community?

Unit reflection

Consider the following statements. Do you agree or disagree with them.
Put a mark on the scale to show how you feel about each statement.
Then write any comments or thoughts you have on the statement below.

1. Your friends and family can help you when you are feeling low or sad.

|⊢————————————————————|————————————————————⊣|

Strongly agree   **Strongly disagree**

_____

_____

2. Spending time with people you care about is important.

|⊢————————————————————|————————————————————⊣|

Strongly agree   **Strongly disagree**

_____

_____

3. Helping others can support your own wellbeing.

|⊢————————————————————|————————————————————⊣|

Strongly agree   **Strongly disagree**

_____

_____

Unit 5.6 Keeping safe

What do you know?

● Where are the different places you go to online and how do you keep yourself safe there?

In this unit, you will:

● Find ways to stay safe online.

● Consider how to keep safe in extreme weather and find out why this is becoming more common.

● Find ways to stay safe when gaming.

Lesson 1 Think before you chat

Activity 6.1a Dangers online

Here are some of the main dangers online. Go through these and rank their seriousness in terms of how dangerous you think they could be from 1 to 10 (with 10 being the most serious). Give your reasons in the final column.

If you are not sure, just go for what you feel is right – your teacher will go through these with you all when you have finished.

Situation	Seriousness (from 1 to 10)	Reason
Sharing your passwords		
Posting things you wouldn't want adults in your life to see		
Clicking on email or message links		
Talking to and trusting people you meet online		
Not covering up your webcam		
Misinformation or fake news		
Sharing or showing personal information		

Lesson 1 Think before you chat

Activity 6.1b Reflection

Reflect on what you have learned in this lesson by answering this question:

How can I keep safe when talking to people online?

You can write your thoughts as bullet points, a mind map or a doodle if you wish, as long as it is easy to understand!

Has anything worried you in this lesson? Write any worries down here so that your teacher can help you.

Is there anything more you would like to know or anything you don't understand?

Lesson 2 It's so hot! It's so cold!

Activity 6.2a Staying safe in the hot and the cold

Draw a person in each bubble.

In one bubble it is a very hot day and the person is ready to stay safe in the heat.

In the other bubble it is a very cold day and the person is ready to stay safe in the cold.

Think about everything you have learned and supply them with everything they will need. You can label your picture too.

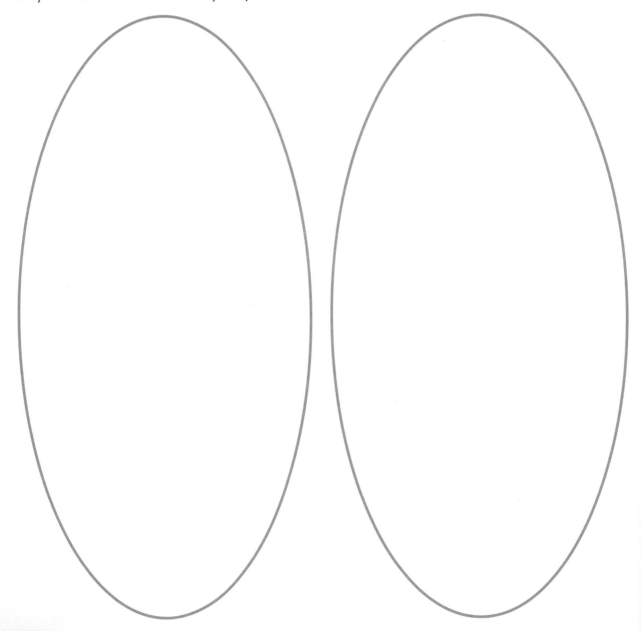

Lesson 2 It's so hot! It's so cold!

Activity 6.2b How we affect the climate and how the climate affects us

Here is some information from a book called *Climate Change: Heatwaves and Big Freezes*. Read the text, then in the space below write down what you understand about the changing world temperatures.

You can also use this space to tell your teacher if there's anything you want more information on.

In the last 120 years, the human population has grown five times larger. To house and feed everyone, many forests have been cut down to build more factories, farms and cities. Billions of humans working, playing and travelling has resulted in more fossil fuels being burnt than ever before.

As a result, we've produced so much carbon dioxide that levels are the highest they've been in 800,000 years!

We also produce another gas called methane. From farming – particularly cows, which burp methane.

These "greenhouse gases" occur naturally too – which is good, because without them Earth would be frozen and lifeless! But current levels are trapping too much heat in our atmosphere.

Lesson 3 Gaming safely

Activity 6.3a Reflection

What have you learned about keeping safe while playing online games?

In the clouds below, draw or write what you remember or what you would like more help with.

Lesson 3 Gaming safely

Activity 6.3b Online all the time

Read this extract from a book called *Hooked*.

10 o'clock The living room. There is an Alyssa-shaped hump under a blanket on the sofa and a glowing light. The door to the living room swings softly open and her dad looks in. He sees the hump and the glowing light.

DAD   What on earth?

Dad steps forward and throws off the blanket.

Alyssa screams in shock.

ALYSSA Dad!! You gave me a heart attack!

DAD [very cross] What are you doing down here? You went to bed an HOUR ago!

ALYSSA I just wanted to finish something.

DAD [looking at the screen] You're watching videos!

ALYSSA They're teaching me how to build archways!

DAD   I don't care, Alyssa, you should be asleep! I don't let you have your computer in your room at night for just this reason! I can't trust you. I had an email from your teacher today saying you hadn't done your homework for the past three weeks. You keep telling me you don't have any – it's a lie! I'm taking these.

He grabs the laptop and headphones.

Alyssa sighs

ALYSSA Fine. I'll finish it tomorrow.

DAD   No, you won't. You're not having these back for a week.

ALYSSA WHAT??

DAD   And you only get them back after that if you can show me some decent manners and catch up on your homework. And eat your dinner and go to bed on time.

ALYSSA Dad, you're totally over-reacting.

DAD   Go back to bed, Alyssa.

Alyssa gets off the sofa and leaves the room, scowling.

Alyssa seems to be getting hooked on things she is watching online. This is a very easy trap to fall into.

If Alyssa was your friend, what would you suggest she could do to break her bad habit?

Unit reflection

What three things do you know about keeping safe now that you have completed this unit?

1
_____
_____
_____
_____

2
_____
_____
_____
_____

3
_____
_____
_____
_____

Is there anything you don't understand or want to learn more about?

_____
_____
_____
_____

Unit 5.7 Changing and learning

What do you know?
- What's happening in this image?
- How can we relate this to our lives?

In this unit, you will:
- Think about how we can change.
- Explore how mistakes can be a good thing.
- Think about how we can think.

Lesson 1 Changes

Activity 7.1a Changes

There are two columns below. Write a list of all the good things you can think of to do with change in the left column, and write all the harder aspects of change that you can think of in the right column.

What's good about change?	What's not so good about change?
● _____	● _____
_____	_____
_____	_____
_____	_____
● _____	● _____
_____	_____
_____	_____
● _____	● _____
_____	_____
_____	_____
● _____	● _____
_____	_____
_____	_____
● _____	● _____
_____	_____
_____	_____

Lesson 1 Changes

Activity 7.1b Poetry notes

Reflect on a change and note down your feelings about it below.

Lesson 2 Problems waiting to be solved

Activity 7.2a Problems waiting to be solved

All of these items below were invented by mistake.

You are going to work as a team and find out how these everyday objects came to be.

Object
1. Chocolate chip cookies
2. Penicillin
3. Cornflakes
4. Playdough
5. Dry cleaning

Object
6. Tyre (vulcanised) rubber
7. Safety pin
8. Crisps (potato chips)
9. Sticky notes
10. Matches

For each one you need to find out:

a) How it was invented (What is the story?)

b) Who invented it and when.

You can present your findings however you would like. Your teacher will provide you with paper, pens and so on.

If you have found out about all of these and still have time, see if you can find out about any more everyday items.

Lesson 2 Problems waiting to be solved

Activity 7.2b Reflection

How can knowing about how everyday objects came about due to mistakes help you when you make mistakes?

Write or draw your thoughts here.

Lesson 3 Brains into action

Activity 7.3a Brain into action plan

- What do I need to do? (assessment)
- What bit can I do well/not so well?
- What can help me? (Any practical resources?)
- How am I going to do it? (This is where you can write a list, sketch some ideas or do a visualisation.)
- Let's start!
- How am I doing? What's going well? Is there anything I need to change?
- When finished, ask: How did I do? (reflection) What went well? What do I need to improve? What can help me?

Use the list above to help you when you are doing your brain games in this lesson.

When you have finished, use this space to write down **what went well with using the list and what you want to work on.**

Remember, this is a skill and, like any skill, the more you practise, the better you get.

Lesson 3 Brains into action

Activity 7.3b Notes

Unit reflection

Think about everything you have learned in this unit, then look again at this image from the introduction.

Imagine this butterfly is worried about the changes that are happening to it. What would you say to this butterfly to help it to change at each stage of its five stages from caterpillar to butterfly?

_____

_____

_____

_____

_____

_____

_____

_____

_____

_____

Unit 5.8 The environment

UNITED NATIONS 🌐 NATIONS UNIES

What do you know?

- Look at the picture of this building. Have you heard of the United Nations? If so, what do you know about it?
- What environmental issues are you aware of?
- What do you already do to help the planet?

In this unit, you will:

- Learn about waste.
- Think about our environmental impact on the planet.

Lesson 1 What can we do to make the world more sustainable?

Activity 8.1a My space for memories and photos!

Stick photos of your swap day on the cork board below.

Lesson 1 What can we do to make the world more sustainable?

Activity 8.1b Reflection

Share your thoughts on the actions you have taken towards living more sustainably as a class.

How was the experience? What did you learn? How did you feel? What more can you do in your own life to support the sustainable goals?

Lesson 2 The Great Pacific Garbage Patch

Activity 8.2a Video notes

While watching 'The Great Pacific Garbage Patch' video, use this page to write notes and facts from the film. You will share these as a class afterwards.

Lesson 2 The Great Pacific Garbage Patch

Activity 8.2b Research

Using the internet, answer these questions about the Great Pacific Garbage Patch. (You can ask your teacher for more paper if you need it.)

1. How big is the Great Pacific Garbage Patch?

2. How much plastic is there estimated to be in this garbage patch?

3. What are the main types of plastic found?

4. Where does the plastic come from?

5. What creatures live among the garbage?

6. Tell me any other interesting facts about the Great Pacific Garbage Patch.

Lesson 3 To travel or not to travel?

Activity 8.3a Debate notes

What were the arguments for and against in your class debate?

_____

_____

_____

_____

_____

_____

_____

_____

_____

_____

_____

_____

What do you think?

_____

_____

_____

_____

_____

_____

_____

_____

_____

_____

_____

Lesson 3 To travel or not to travel?

Activity 8.3b Challenge: Can you draw the planet?

Unit reflection

In this unit you have learned about doing your bit for sustainability, about the Great Pacific Garbage Patch and you have debated the pros and cons of travelling.

Reflect back on this learning and, below, write or draw and label the key things you have learned.

Is there anything else you would like to learn or do not understand? Write these down so that your teacher can help you.

Acknowledgements

We are grateful to the following for permission to reproduce copyright material:

4.1.3. Cover image from *The Thing Lou Couldn't Do* written and illustrated by Ashley Spires, cover illustration © 2017 Ashley Spires. Reproduced by permission of Kids Can Press Ltd., Toronto. **5.4.3**, An extract about bullying, NSPCC, https://www.nspcc.org.uk/what-is-child-abuse/types-of-abuse/bullying-and-cyberbullying/. Reproduced with permission; **5.6.3**, "Game age ratings explained", PEGI, copyright © PEGI S.A. Reproduced with permission; and **5.7.2**, Quotes by Sir James Dyson, https://www.dyson.com/james-dyson, copyright © Sir James Dyson, 2011-2023. Reproduced with kind permission.

The Publishers wish to thank the following for permission to reproduce images and copyright material. Every effort has been made to trace copyright holders and to obtain their permission for the use of copyright materials. The publishers will gladly receive any information enabling them to rectify any error or omission at the first opportunity.

4.1.1 SB p. 1 (tl) Vector bucket/ Shutterstock, (tr) StudioBrandShop/ Shutterstock, 4.1.1 (bl) ober-art / Shutterstock, (br) Vector bucket/ Shutterstock, 4.1.1 PPT Slide 1 MillaF/Shutterstock, Slide 3 & SB p. 2 jsabirova/Shutterstock, Slide 4 violetkaipa/Shutterstock, Slide 5 Yury Zap/ Shutterstock, WS 4.1.1a jsabirova/Shutterstock, **4.1.2** PPT Slide 1 Ground Picture/ Shutterstock, Slide 2 (l) PeopleImages.com – Yuri A/ Shutterstock, (tr) Roman Samborskyi/ Shutterstock, (br) anut21ng Stock/ Shutterstock, Slide 3 Gelpi/Shutterstock, Slide 4 YASH GARG FOTOGRAFIE/ Shutterstock, WS 4.1.2b YASH GARG FOTOGRAFIE/ Shutterstock, **4.1.3** PPT Slide 1 & SB p. 8 MinskDesign/ Shutterstock, Slide 2 Cover image from The Thing Lou Couldn't Do written and illustrated by Ashley Spires, cover illustration © 2017 Ashley Spires. Reproduced by permission of Kids Can Press Ltd., Toronto. **4.2.1** PPT Slide 5 Oleg Nesterov/ Shutterstock, Slides 1-5 Reprinted by permission of HarperCollins Publishers Ltd © 2023, Lisa Rajan, **4.2.2** Ealita.ID/ Shutterstock, SB p14 Ealita.ID/ Shutterstock, SB p. 15 Nicoleta Ionescu/ Shutterstock, **4.2.3** WS Nicoleta Ionescu/Shutterstock, PPT Slide 1 Iconic Bestiary/ Shutterstock, Slide 2 (tl) Moosavefoto/ Shutterstock, (t) Monkey Business Images/ Shutterstock, (tr) Africa Studio/ Shutterstock, (bl) Shyamalamuralinath/ Shutterstock, (br) Jacob Lund/ Shutterstock, Slide 3 (tl) Patrick Foto/Shutterstock, (tr) Elena Yakusheva/Shutterstock, (bl) Govind Jangvir/Shutterstock, (br) Daria Medvedeva/Shutterstock, **4.3.1** WS 4.3.1a Jr images/ Shutterstock, SB p. 17 RomanR/ Shutterstock, PPT Slide 1 Tatjana Baibakova/ Shutterstock, Slide 3 Kaspars Grinvalds/ Shutterstock, Slide 7 & SB pp20–21 NIPAPORN PANYACHAROEN/ Shutterstock, Slide 7 & SB pp20–21 MarcoFood/ Shutterstock, Slide 7 & SB pp20–21 Tim UR/ Shutterstock, Slide 7 & SB pp20–21 Ermak Oksana/ Shutterstock, Slide 7 & SB pp20–21 Dionisvera/ Shutterstock, Slide 7 & SB pp20–21 baibaz/ Shutterstock, Slide 7 & SB pp20–21 Craevschii Family/ Shutterstock, Slide 7 & SB pp20–21 New Africa/ Shutterstock, **4.3.2** PPT Slide 1 (r) Daxiao Productions/ Shutterstock, (l) RomanR/ Shutterstock, Slide 2 & SB p. 23 Benjamin Ordaz/ Shutterstock, Slides 3 & 6 inspiring.team/ Shutterstock, SB 4.3.2 inspiring.team/ Shutterstock, **4.3.3** PPT Slide 1 (b) Riccardo Mayer/ Shutterstock, (tl) PeopleImages.com – Yuri A/ Shutterstock, (tr) aslysun/ Shutterstock, Slide 3 Ory Gonian/ Shutterstock, Slide 4 riopatuca/ Shutterstock, Slide 6 yusufdemirci/ Shutterstock, **4.4.1** SB p. 25 (t) Monkey Business Images/Shutterstock, p. 25 (r) Rohit Seth/Shutterstock, p. 25 (b) Monkey Business Images/Shutterstock, p. 26 Athanasia Nomikou/ Shutterstock, **4.4.2** SB p. 28 Athanasia Nomikou/ Shutterstock, WS 4.4.2 Athanasia Nomikou/ Shutterstock, PPT Slide 1 (tl) Sophon Nawit/ Shutterstock, (tr) Rawpixel.com/ Shutterstock, (bl) Denis Kuvaev/ Shutterstock, (br) Ground Picture/ Shutterstock, Slide 2 wavebreakmedia/ Shutterstock, Slide 3 (tl) Prostock-studio/ Shutterstock, (t) Ground Picture/ Shutterstock, (tr) mguttman/ Shutterstock, (bl) Darrin Henry/ Shutterstock, (b) Monkey Business Images/ Shutterstock, (bl) Reshetnikov_art/ Shutterstock, Slide 4 Monkey Business Images/ Shutterstock, **4.4.3** PPT Slides 1 & 2 Rawpixel.com/ Shutterstock, slides 3 & 4 Lemberg Vector studio/ Shutterstock, Slide 5 Dmitry Demidovich / Shutterstock, Slide 6 theshots.co/ Shutterstock, SB p. 32 Svetliy/ Shutterstock, **4.5.1** SB p. 33 (tl) dzejdi/ Shutterstock, (tr) IZZ HAZEL/ Shutterstock, (bl) nikolae/ Shutterstock, (br) TotemArt/ Shutterstock, PPT Slide 4 Ken Cook/ Shutterstock, **4.5.2** PPT Slide 3 ESB Professional/ Shutterstock, Slide 4 & SB p. 36 OlyaOK/ Shutterstock, pp. 37 & 40 Eightshot_Studio / Shutterstock, SB Eightshot_Studio / Shutterstock, **4.5.3** PPT Slide 1 (br) Africa Studio/Adobe Stock, (tr) ilikestudio/ Shutterstock, (bl) vesna cvorovic / Shutterstock, (tl) UfaBizPhoto/ Shutterstock, Slide 2 Littlekidmoment/ Shutterstock, Slide 3 Elena_Dig / Shutterstock, Slide 4 & SB p. 39 Luis Molinero/ Shutterstock, Slide 5 Thinglass / Shutterstock, Slide 6 New Africa / Shutterstock, **4.6.1** SB p41 (tl) cunaplus/ Shutterstock, (tr) Dinesh Hukmani/ Shutterstock, (bl) Fedor Selivanov/ Shutterstock, (br) Motortion Films/ Shutterstock, PPT Slide 1 Kirk Fisher/ Shutterstock, Slides 2 & 5 Gina Kelly / Alamy Stock Photo, **4.6.2** PPT Slide 1 (tl) nik_nadal/ Shutterstock, (tr) ADM Photo / Shutterstock, (bl) fotokaleinar / Shutterstock, (br) vchal / Shutterstock, Slide 2 mindscanner/ Shutterstock, **4.6.3** SB p. 46 hurricanehank/ Shutterstock, WS 4.6.3 hurricanehank/ Shutterstock, PPT Slide 1 Prostock-studio/ Shutterstock, Slide 2 Prostock-studio / Shutterstock, Slide 4 Monkey Business Images / Shutterstock, **4.7.1** SB p. 49 & PPT 4.7.2 Slide 1 (tr) Roman Samborskyi/ Shutterstock, 4.7.1 SB pp. 49 & 54, ChristianChan / Shutterstock, SB p. 49& 4.7.1 PPT Slide 1 imtmphoto / Shutterstock, 4.7.1 PPT Slide 2 Erik Clegg / Shutterstock, 4.7.1 PPT Slide 3 WESTOCK PRODUCTIONS / Shutterstock, 4.7.1 PPT Slide 4 designkida / Shutterstock, 4.7.1 PPT Slide 5 Nach-Noth / Shutterstock, **4.7.2** PPT Slide 1 (l) ChristianChan / Shutterstock, (br) Dina Belenko/ Shutterstock, Slide 2 & SB p. 53 Zainudin_Kho / Shutterstock, WS 4.7.2 Zainudin_Kho / Shutterstock, **4.7.3** PPT Slide 1 Prostock-studio/ Shutterstock,

Slide 2 boxstock / Shutterstock, **4.8.1** SB p. 57 max dallocco/ Shutterstock, PPT slide 1 Preres/ Shutterstock, slide 2 Prapat Aowsakorn/ Shutterstock, slide 3 Studio_G/ Shutterstock, SB p. 58, PPT, WS Studio_G/ Shutterstock, **4.8.2** PPT slide 1 & SB p59 © HarperCollins Publisher 2020, slides 2 & 3 (tl) AlenKadr/ Shutterstock, slides 2 & 3 (tr) Teerasak Ladnongkhun/ Shutterstock, slides 2 & 3 (bl) Mike Truchon/ Shutterstock 4.8.2 (br) M88/ Shutterstock, slide 5 Part of Design/ Shutterstock, SB p. 60 (t) frank60/ Shutterstock, (b) Rich Carey/ Shutterstock, SB p. 61 Maryshot/ Shutterstock, **4.8.3** PPT Slide 1 Lightspring/ Shutterstock, **5.1.1** SB p. 1 (tl) Atomic Roderick/ Shutterstock, (tr) Jasmine Creation/ Shutterstock, (b) mentalmind/ Shutterstock, PPT Slide 1 asiandelight/ Shutterstock, Slide 2 Michael Kraus/ Shutterstock, **5.1.2** PPT Slide 1 (l) Sabrina Bracher/ Shutterstock, (r) Queenmoonlite Studio/ Shutterstock, Slide 2 Natalie Board/ Shutterstock, Slide 3 Andrekart Photography/ Shutterstock, Slide 4 Chay_Tee/ Shutterstock, Slide 5 © HarperCollins Publishers 2020, **5.1.3** SB p.6 HowLettery/Shutterstock, p.7 CallMeTak/ Shutterstock WS HowLettery/Shutterstock, PPT Slide 1 Rambleron/Vecteezy, Slide 2 (t) Ground Picture/ Shutterstock, (bl) Godong/ Alamy Stock Photo, (br) James Kirkikis/ Shutterstock, Slide 3 Microstocker.Pro/ Shutterstock, Slide 4 GoodStudio/ Shutterstock, Slide 4 TALVA/ Shutterstock, **5.2.1** SB p.9 KlingSup/ Shutterstock, PPT Slide 1 Kolonko/ Shutterstock, Slide 2 metamorworks/ Shutterstock, Slide 3 Ground Picture/ Shutterstock, Slide 4 (tl) minizen/ Shutterstock, (t) Net Vector/ Shutterstock, (tr) giedre vaitekune/ Shutterstock, (bl) Yuri Chuprakov/ Shutterstock, (b) Simakova Mariia/ Shutterstock, (br) backUp/ Shutterstock, **5.2.2** PPT Slide 1 Kaspars Grinvalds/Shutterstock, Slide 2 Vladimir Gjorgiev/ Shutterstock, Slide 3 Africa Studio/ Shutterstock, Slide 4 Mariia Boiko/ Shutterstock, Slide 5 Nor Gal/ Shutterstock, SB p.13 karakotsya/ Shutterstock, **5.2.3** PPT Slide 1 (l) & SB p.16 Viktorija Reuta/ Shutterstock, Slide 1 (r) maglyvi/ Shutterstock, Slide 2 & 3 Daisy Daisy/ Shutterstock, Slide 2 + 3 Timolina/ Shutterstock, Slide 2 + 3 Hung Chung Chih/ Shutterstock, Slide 2 + 3 alif_Osman/ Shutterstock, Slide 2 + 3 ESB Professional/ Shutterstock, Slide 3 Wahyu Ananda/ Shutterstock, Slide 3 wavebreakmedia/ Shutterstock, Slide 4 (l) stockpexel/ Shutterstock, (r) wavebreakmedia/ Shutterstock, Slide 4 PeopleImages.com – Yuri A/ Shutterstock, SB p.15 (l) Aleksandr Merg/ Shutterstock, WS 5.2.3a Aleksandr Merg/ Shutterstock, SB p. 15 (r) woocat/ Shutterstock, WS 5.2.3a woocat/ Shutterstock, WS 5.2.3b, SB p.16 Viktorija Reuta/Shutterstock, **5.3.1** SB p.17 (tl) pixelheadphoto digitalskillet/ Shutterstock, (tr) F01 PHOTO/ Shutterstock, (b) fizkes/ Shutterstock, PPT Slide 1 (l) fizkes/ Shutterstock, (r) Nowaczyk/ Shutterstock, Slide 2 (l) SeventyFour/ Shutterstock, (r) Solid photos/ Shutterstock, Slide 3 (tl) fizkes/ Shutterstock, (r) Krakenimages.com/ Shutterstock, (bl) MalikNalik/ Shutterstock, SB p.18 (t) & PPT Slide 4 PixyPen/ Shutterstock, TG WS PixyPen/ Shutterstock, SB p.18 (b) Colorfuel Studio/ Shutterstock, TG WS Colorfuel Studio/ Shutterstock, **5.3.2** PPT Slide 1 ANURAK PONGPATIMET/ Shutterstock, Slide 2 + 3 (bl) Lakmal Ditmax/ Shutterstock, PPT Slide 2 (tr) Lapina/ Shutterstock, Slide 2 (br) New Africa/ Shutterstock, Slide 3 (t) Carkhe/ Shutterstock, (l) Kolonko/ Shutterstock, TG WS 5.3.2, **5.3.3** PPT Slide 1 (b) WEB-DESIGN/ Shutterstock, Slide 3 Studio Barcelona/ Shutterstock, Slide 5 Frenggo/ Shutterstock, PPT Slide 6 katsuba_art/Shutterstock, **5.4.1** SB p.25 Rawpixel.com/ Shutterstock, p.26 Vegorus/ Shutterstock, WS Vegorus/ Shutterstock,SB p.27 Monkey Business Images/ Shutterstock, PPT Slide 1 (tl) IndianFaces/ Shutterstock, (tr) SALMONNEGRO-STOCK/ Shutterstock, (bl) Aleem Zahid Khan/ Shutterstock, (br) Yuri Dondish/ Shutterstock, Slide 3 wellphoto/ Shutterstock, **5.4.2** PPT Slide 1 & SB p.29 afry_harvy/ Shutterstock, Slide 2 Pressmaster/ Shutterstock, Slide 3 LightField Studios/ Shutterstock, SB p.30 Reprinted by permission of HarperCollins Publishers Ltd © 2022 A. M. Dassu, **5.4.3** PPT Slides 4–6 Intellson/ Shutterstock, **5.5.1** SB p.33 SewCreamStudio/ Shutterstock, PPT Slide 2 (tl) Prostock-studio/ Shutterstock, (tr) HAKINMHAN/ Shutterstock, (bl) Image bug/ Shutterstock, (br) pixelheadphoto digitalskillet/ Shutterstock, Slide 3 vectornation/ Shutterstock, Slide 4 Pixel-Shot/ Shutterstock, **5.5.2** PPT Slide 1 (tl) memej/ Shutterstock, (t) Yukhym Turkin/ Shutterstock, (tr) Aletkina Olga/ Shutterstock, (bl) Glinskaja Olga/ Shutterstock, (br) woocat/Shutterstock, Slide 2 Sudowoodo/ Shutterstock, Slide 4 MARI_NAD/ Shutterstock, **5.5.3** PPT Slide 1 & SB p.37 Elena Zajchikova/ Shutterstock, Slide 2 tangguhpro/ Shutterstock, Slide 3 Seqoya/ Shutterstock, Slide 4 & SB p.38 Victoria 1/ Shutterstock, SB p.38 Maksym Drozd/ Shutterstock, **5.6.1** SB p.41 WESTOCK PRODUCTIONS/ Shutterstock, PPT Slide 3 & SB p.42 Pungu x/ Shutterstock, WS Pungu x/ Shutterstock, PPT Slide 5 Pixel-Shot/ Shutterstock, Slide 6 Roman Arbuzov/ Shutterstock, **5.6.2** SB p.45 (t) TR STOK/ Shutterstock, (b) Gatien GREGORI/ Shutterstock, SB p.45 Text Reprinted by permission of HarperCollins Publishers Ltd © 2022 Mio Debnam, PPT Slide 1 trgrowth/ Shutterstock, Slide 2 Phonix_a Pk.sarote/ Shutterstock, Slide 3 Pakhnyushchy/ Shutterstock, Slide 4 kornnphoto/ Shutterstock, Slide 5 Dmitry Naumov/ Shutterstock, Slide 6 AntiD/ Shutterstock, **5.6.3** SB p.47 Reprinted by permission of HarperCollins Publishers Ltd © 2023 Jo Cotterill, SB p.48 (t) Monster Ztudio/ Shutterstock, (l) Rafael Croonen/ Shutterstock, (b) Luce Altra/ Shutterstock, PPT Slide 1 SynthEx/ Shutterstock, Slide 2 HamaVision/Shutterstock, Slide 3 (tr) smx12/Shutterstock, (r) Oleksandra Klestova/ Shutterstock, (br) Toxa2x2/ Shutterstock, Slide 4 Aleksandra Suzi/ Shutterstock, **5.7.1** SB pp. 49&56 Darkdiamond67/ Shutterstock, PPT Slide 1 Food Impressions/ Shutterstock, Slide 3 winyuu/ Shutterstock, Slide 4 Petar Dojranliev/ Shutterstock, **5.7.2** SB p.53 GoodStudio/ Shutterstock, PPT Slide 1 Olena Yakobchuk/ Shutterstock, Slide 3 (tl) Winai Tepsuttinun/ Shutterstock, (t) Elnur/ Shutterstock, (l) luchschenF/ Shutterstock, (t) rvlsoft/ Shutterstock, (c) Passakorn sakulphan/ Shutterstock, (r) Ilina Yuliia/ Shutterstock, (tr) Sergio33/ Shutterstock, (bl) Volodymyr Krasyuk/ Shutterstock, (b) Pixel-Shot/ Shutterstock, (br) Chonlatee42/ Shutterstock, Slide 4 horst friedrichs / Alamy Stock Photo, **5.7.3** PPT Slide 1 ImageFlow/ Shutterstock, Slide 4 Serhii Bobyk/ Shutterstock, Slide 5 Red Fox studio/ Shutterstock, **5.8.1** SB p.57 nexus 7/ Shutterstock, p.58 piotr_pabijan/ Shutterstock, p59 &

PPT Slide 1 MintBlac/ Shutterstock, Slide 2 checy/ Shutterstock, Slide 3 Monster Ztudio/ Shutterstock, Slide 4 (tr) rtbilder/ Shutterstock, (l) Ugis Riba/ Shutterstock, (br) Pakphoom9/ Shutterstock, **5.8.2** SB p.60 & PPT Slide 1 Shane Gross/ Shutterstock, Slide 2 Elime/ Shutterstock, **5.8.3** SB p.62 BearFotos/ Shutterstock, WS BearFotos/ Shutterstock, PPT Slide 1 (t) Paolo Bona/ Shutterstock, (bl) Dani Vincek/ Shutterstock (br) Tae PY15MU/ Shutterstock, Slide 2 (t) WitR/ Shutterstock, (bl) Melnikov Dmitriy/ Shutterstock, (br) aphotostory/ Shutterstock, Slide 3 & SB p. 64 Dmitrijs Mihejevs/ Shutterstock, Slide 5 (l) Johny Bayu Fitantra/ Shutterstock, (r) j.chizhe/ Shutterstock, **6.1.1** SB p.1 F01 PHOTO/ Shutterstock, p.2 Asti Mak/ Shutterstock, p.3 (t) Roman Samborskyi/ Shutterstock, (b) Prostock-studio/ Shutterstock, PPT Slide 1 Marish/ Shutterstock, Slide 3 & SB p.7 Dmytro Onopko/ Shutterstock, Slide 4 (l) marekuliasz/ Shutterstock, (tr) Ronnachai Palas/ Shutterstock, (tb) CREATISTA/ Shutterstock, **6.1.2** SB p.5 (t) JPC-PROD/ Shutterstock, (b) Veja/ Shutterstock, PPT Slide 1 Text Reprinted by permission of HarperCollins Publishers Ltd © 2023 Kathryn Kendall Boucher, Slide 1 S K Chavan/ Shutterstock, Slide 2 (t) Ground Picture/ Shutterstock, Slide 2 (l) Ground Picture/ Shutterstock, (r) Creativa Images/ Shutterstock, slide 3 Esteban De Armas/ Shutterstock, Slide 4 Just dance/ Shutterstock, **6.1.3** PPT Slide 1 (l) Anastasia Shilova/ Shutterstock, (tr) MIA Studio/ Shutterstock, (br) Elena Nichizhenova/ Shutterstock, Slide 2 VectorPlotnikoff/ Shutterstock, Slide 3 Nicoleta Ionescu/ Shutterstock, SB p. 7 Vector bucket/ Shutterstock, Yayayoyo/ Shutterstock, Yayayoyo/ Shutterstock, Vector bucket/ Shutterstock, Yayayoyo/ Shutterstock, Dmytro Onopko/ Shutterstock, p.8 IYIKON/ Shutterstock, **6.2.1** SB p.9 Dejan Dundjerski/ Shutterstock, PPT Slide 1 (l) pathdoc/ Shutterstock, (r) pathdoc/ Shutterstock, Slide 2 (l) imtmphoto/ Shutterstock, (r) Monkey Business Images/ Shutterstock, Slide 3 (tl) cdrin/ Shutterstock, (tr) fizkes/ Shutterstock, (bl) lovelyday12/ Shutterstock, (br) Pressmaster/ Shutterstock, Slide 4 & SB p.11 Brian A Jackson/ Shutterstock, Slide 5 &SB p.11 Arcady/ Shutterstock, Slide 6 & SB p.11 Yuganov Konstantin/ Shutterstock, **6.2.2** SB p.12 T. Lesia/ Shutterstock, PPT Slide 2 Khoroshunova Olga/ Shutterstock, Slide 4 xtock/ Shutterstock, **6.2.3** PPT Slide 1 (tl) Stock Exchange/ Shutterstock, (tr) TinnaPong/ Shutterstock, (bl) jianbing Lee/ Shutterstock, (br) vivanvu/ Shutterstock, 6.2.3PPT Slide 3 (tl) Laboo Studio/ Shutterstock, (t) matimix/ Shutterstock, (bl) wavebreakmedia/ Shutterstock, (br) Jose Gil/ Shutterstock, (tr) M Stocker/ Shutterstock, Slide 4 Pressmaster/ Shutterstock, SB p.16 (b) Zoart Studio/ Shutterstock, (t)Vitalii Petrenko/ Shutterstock, WS 6.3.1 p.129 Zoart Studio/ Shutterstock, **6.3.1** SB p.18 Zoart Studio/ Shutterstock, p.17 Jeruik/ Shutterstock, PPT Slide 3 Andrii Yalanskyi/ Shutterstock, **6.3.2** PPT Slide 1 (tl) javi_indy/ Shutterstock, (tr) Monkey Business Images/ Shutterstock, (bl) Pressmaster/ Shutterstock, (br) pixelheadphoto digitalskillet/ Shutterstock, Slide 2 & SB p. 24 Iconic Bestiary/ Shutterstock, Slide 3 German Vizulis/Shutterstock, Slide 4 Pictorial Press Ltd / Alamy Stock Photo, Slide 5 (t) Chronicle / Alamy Stock Photo, (b) Reprinted by permission of HarperCollins Publishers Ltd © 2013 Anne Rooney, SB p.21 wavebreakmedia/ Shutterstock, **6.3.3** SB p.22 UnderhilStudio/ Shutterstock, p. 23 Oxy_gen/ Shutterstock , WS 6.3.3 UnderhilStudio/ Shutterstock, PPT Slide 1 (l) Tanya Antusenok/ Shutterstock, (r) Piotr Urakau/ Shutterstock, Slides 2 &3 Fotomay/ Shutterstock, Slide 4 Natata/ Shutterstock, **6.4.1** SB pp.25&32 AMR Studio/ Shutterstock, PPT Slide 2 Colored Lights/ Shutterstock, **6.4.2** PPT Slides 2&6 Ruslana Iurchenko/ Shutterstock, Slides 3&6 (r) A Sharma/ Shutterstock, Slide 3 (l) LightField Studios/ Shutterstock, Slide 4 SynthEx/ Shutterstock, **6.4.3** PPT Slide 1 Alina Reynbakh/ Shutterstock, Slide 3 TungCheung/ Shutterstock, Slide 5 Olivier Le Moal/ Shutterstock, SB p.30 Nata Bene/ Shutterstock, **6.5.1** SB p.33 Rawpixel.com/ Shutterstock, p.34 Rudie Strummer/ Shutterstock, PPT Slide 1 Yuliya Chsherbakova/ Shutterstock, Slide 2 WESTOCK PRODUCTIONS/ Shutterstock, Slide 3 marekuliasz/ Shutterstock, **6.5.2** PPT Slide 1 (TL) Kehinde Temitope Odutayo/ Shutterstock, (tr) CHEN WS/ Shutterstock, (bl) arun sambhu mishra/ Shutterstock, (b) Free Wind 2014/ Shutterstock (br) Lewis Tse/ Shutterstock, Slide 2 (tl) ESB Professional/ Shutterstock, (tr) Daniel M Ernst/ Shutterstock, (bl) Anirut Thailand/ Shutterstock, (br) MUHAMMAD IZZAT TERMIZIE/ Shutterstock, Slide 4 (tl) Monkey Business Images/ Shutterstock, (tr) BRAIN2HANDS/ Shutterstock, (b) Evgeny Atamanenko/ Shutterstock, **6.5.3** PPT Slides 1 + 2 ssguy/ Shutterstock, Slide 3 SALMONNEGRO-STOCK/ Shutterstock, Slide 4 Ronnachai Palas/ Shutterstock, Slide 5 (tr) Sabrina Bracher/ Shutterstock, (tl) oneinchpunch/ Shutterstock, (t) Kristof Bellens/ Shutterstock, (bl) Sarawut Chamsaeng/ Shutterstock, (br) imtmphoto/ Shutterstock, Slide 7 justaa/ Shutterstock, SB p.39 Nizwa Design/ Shutterstock, **6.6.1** SB p.41 (tl) Antlii/ Shutterstock, (r) maicasaa/ Shutterstock, (bl) omphoto/ Shutterstock, SB p.42 & PPT slide 2 Vitalii Vodolazskyi/ Shutterstock, WS 6.6.1 Vitalii Vodolazskyi/ Shutterstock, PPT Slide 1 13_Phunkod/ Shutterstock, Slide 3 512r/ Shutterstock, **6.6.2** PPT Slide 1 elenabsl/ Shutterstock, Slide 2 Standard Studio/ Shutterstock, SB p.44/ PPT Slide 4 EreborMountain/Shutterstock, SB p.45 Reprinted by permission of HarperCollins Publishers Ltd © 2020 Lisa Rajan, **6.6.3** PPT Slide 1 & SB p.46 desdemona72/ Shutterstock, **6.7.1** SB p.49 Jacques Paganel/ Shutterstock, PPT Slide 1 Viacheslav Lopatin/Shutterstock, Slide 2 GoodStudio/ Shutterstock, Slide 3 &SB p. 50 (t) Vasilinka/ Shutterstock, Slide 3 & SB p.50 (b) Bibadash/ Shutterstock, SB p.51 Simakova Mariia/ Shutterstock, WS 6.7.1, **6.7.2** PPT Slide 1 Sipa/Shutterstock, Slide 3 Gustavo Frazao/ Shutterstock, **6.7.3** PPT Slide 1 Vgstockstudio/ Shutterstock, Slide 3 Gorodenkoff/ Shutterstock, SB p.56 Christina Designs/ Shutterstock, **6.8.1** SB p.57 Nostalgia for Infinity/ Shutterstock, PPT Slide 1 (tl) Ermolaev Alexander/ Shutterstock, (tr) DisobeyArt/ Shutterstock, (br) rangizzz/ Shutterstock, (bl) Diyana Dimitrova/ Shutterstock, Slide 2 Tang Yan Song/ Shutterstock, Slide 3 (tl) Marquess789/ Shutterstock, (tr) Vitalii Karas/ Shutterstock, (bl) lovelyday12/ Shutterstock, (br) Sergey Ryzhov/ Shutterstock, **6.8.2** PPT Slide 2 Thinglass/ Shutterstock, Slide 3 Photo_Pix/ Shutterstock, **6.8.3**SB p.63 Lightspring/ Shutterstock, p.64 phloxii/ Shutterstock, WS 6.8.2 Simakova Mariia/ Shutterstock